Brachiosaurus

Brachiosaurus

Heather Amery

Illustrated by Tony Gibbons

DINOSAUR COLLECTION

PARRAGON

Contents

Introducing Brachiosaurus

Brachiosaurus 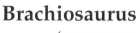 (<u>BRACK</u>-EE-OH-<u>SAW</u>-RUS) was a giant. It was one of the biggest and heaviest dinosaurs that ever lived. It was also one of the tallest, with an enormously long neck with which it could reach right up to the tree tops. A giraffe – if it had existed in Jurassic times – would only have reached up to its shoulders. And by stretching up, you would hardly have been able to touch even its knees.

It lived about 145 million years ago.

Its bones have been found in those parts of the world that are now the United States and parts of Africa.

Brachiosaurus  means 'arm lizard'. It was given this name because its front legs, unlike those of most dinosaurs, were longer than its back ones. In many ways, both the front and back legs were like pillars, supporting its tremendous body weight.

How much do scientists know about **Brachiosaurus?** Turn the pages that follow to find out all about this long-necked dinosaur.

Towering monster

Brachiosaurus' neck was so long that, if it were not extinct, it could look over the roof of a three-storey house. From its snout to the end of its powerful tail, it was as long as a tennis court. And it weighed as much as several fully-grown elephants.

It had massive stumpy legs to carry its body weight of up to 70 tonnes, and short, thick toes. Underneath each foot was a thick pad which protected its bones from jarring on the ground as it walked.

Because it was so big, **Brachiosaurus** could not move as quickly as some smaller dinosaurs. But it had a long stride and so covered huge distances fairly quickly. If you had been able to stand next to a **Brachiosaurus,** it would have towered high above you.

Brachiosaurus would sway its neck about and turn its head from side to side when feeding. It must also have had a very large and powerful heart to pump blood all the way up its long neck to its brain.

Some scientists have suggested it may have had a specially designed heart to help circulate its blood all round its enormous body. Others think it may even have had two hearts to help with this work.

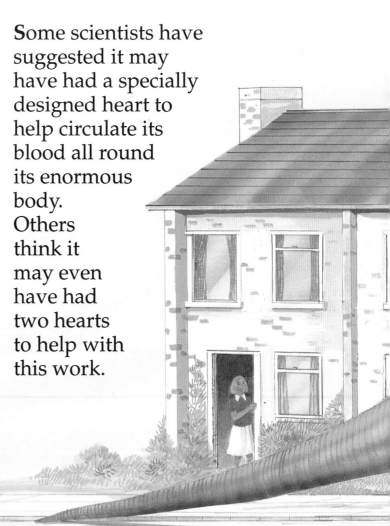

But although **Brachiosaurus** was so big, its head was small and broad, and it had a very small brain for the size of its body. Its nostrils were very large and on top of its head.

Brachiosaurus' neck operated very much like a crane does today and was moved by a system of ribs and powerful muscles. The bones in its neck were light in weight, so that it could raise and lower the neck quite easily.

At first, it was thought that **Brachiosaurus** might have had a trunk, like the elephants we know today. But scientists do not think so now.

7

Long-necked skeleton

Brachiosaurus had a very strong framework of bones to hold up its enormous body. The most noticeable thing about its skeleton is its long neck.

Balancing this great neck was a long tail. **Brachiosaurus** could lash its tail from side to side, and probably raised it off the ground when walking.

Its legs were very powerful and thick, like an elephant's. The front legs were longer than the back ones. On each of its broad feet it had five short toes.

Brachiosaurus ate so much that it had a huge gut.

It therefore needed to support all this weight on all four, sturdy legs. **Brachiosaurus** probably could not rear up on its back legs like some dinosaurs. But its neck was so long that it would not have needed to do this anyway.

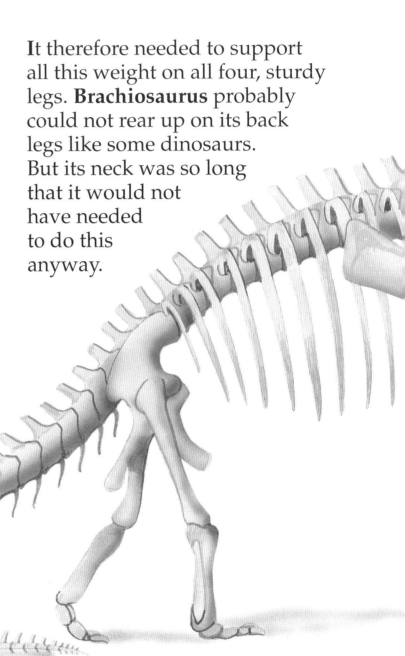

Notice how its massive backbone was arched to hold up the weight of its enormous body.

Brachiosaurus was so strong that it might even have been able to carry almost half its own weight – perhaps as much as 30 tonnes – on its back.

Scientists once thought that **Brachiosaurus** probably lived in lakes and rivers. They imagined that the water would have helped to hold up its huge body and that it could have fed on soft water plants.

As **Brachiosaurus** walked, it must have held its legs very straight. It was so heavy that, if it had bent its legs a lot, the bones might have broken under all that weight.

Attached to the backbone were long rib bones, protecting its lungs and stomach.

Muscles that stretched from its back and right up its neck were useful in helping **Brachiosaurus** to hold up its head without too much of an effort.

Now, however, scientists believe that it lived for most of the time on land, only occasionally paddling in water. If it had lived all the time in water, its ribs might have been crushed by the weight of the water and it would not have been able to breathe easily.

Notice how small the skull seems when you compare it with the rest of **Brachiosaurus'** body. But it was actually longer than your arm.

9

African discovery

One of the biggest and most complete dinosaur skeletons ever found was of a **Brachiosaurus**.

A German scientist, who was hunting for minerals in Tanzania, Africa, about 85 years ago, came across some huge bones at a place called Tendaguru.

He reported his remarkable find, and soon a dig was organized.

The African dig lasted for four years. There was a lot of hard work to be done.

All the bones found then had to be carried to the nearest port, over 65 kilometres away. Altogether, the men helping on the dig made over 5,000 trips to the port, and carried 250 tonnes of dinosaur bones.

Among all those bones that were shipped out of Africa were those of a **Brachiosaurus.** The gigantic rebuilt skeleton is now on view in a museum in Berlin, Germany, where it has pride of place.

It has been described as the most impressive dinosaur skeleton in the world, standing 12m tall and all of 22.5m long.

Jurassic life

Herds of **Brachiosaurus** roamed plains and forests about 160 – 145 million years ago, in the Jurassic Period. Browsing on the tallest trees, they trampled great paths through the ferns which grew thickly on the ground, leaving trails of footprints and droppings.

At that time, the weather was warm and damp.

The first birds flew overhead, and huge pterosaurs flapped through the air on leathery wings.

Herds of **Brachiosaurus** were always on the look-out for meat-eating dinosaurs.

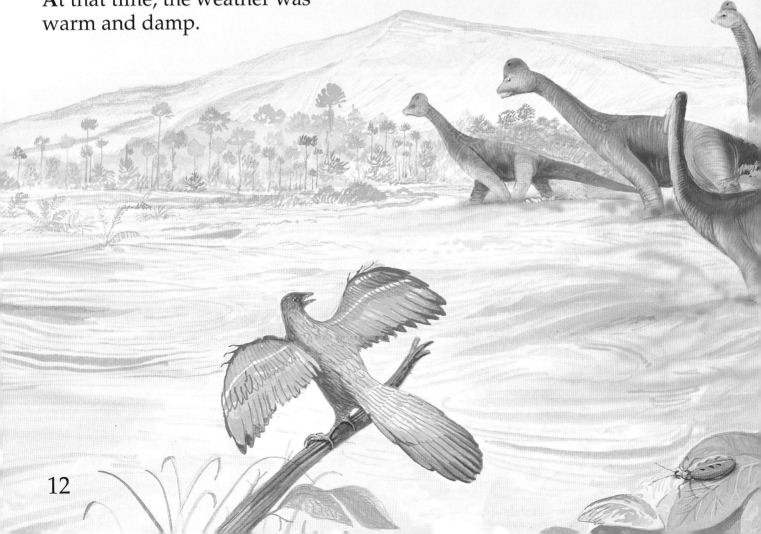

13

Massive meals

Brachiosaurus only ate plants. With its long neck, it could feed on the tallest trees, picking off leaves and twigs for its meals. These were too high for other plant-eating dinosaurs to reach.

Some scientists think that **Brachiosaurus** also browsed on water plants, stretching its neck down to feed from the banks of rivers or lakes.

It must have eaten a huge amount of food for enough energy to power its massive body. An elephant eats about 150 kilos of food a day. **Brachiosaurus**, ten times bigger, needed a great deal more.

Because of the tremendous amount of leaves and plants that **Brachiosaurus** ate every day, scientists think that its droppings must have been the most enormous heaps!

After **Brachiosaurus** had gulped down its food, special muscles pounded the plants to a mush between rough pebbles that the dinosaur had swallowed for this purpose.

15

Life in the herd

Brachiosaurus probably lived in family groups or small herds of up to twenty dinosaurs.

As the fully-grown adults were so large and needed so much food, the herd may have moved on to find new grazing grounds each day.

When they had stripped all the leaves off the tops of one clump of trees, they wandered on to the next clump and fed there, too. They did not bother about leaves further down the tree. It would have been a strain on their necks, so lower leaves were left for smaller dinosaurs to browse on.

As the herds travelled, the young dinosaurs were watched and guarded by the large adults who left the huge, deep footprints in the soft ground that still exist today.

When threatened by a big meat-eating dinosaur hunting for a meal, the young would run to their mothers for safety. The big males may then have surrounded the rest of the herd to protect them from a predatory carnivore.

A newly-hatched **Brachiosaurus** was probably only as big as a dog. Scientists think it had a soft skin at first which became tough and scaly as it grew older.

It may have taken very many years before a **Brachiosaurus** grew into a full-sized adult and was ready to mate and have its own young.

The sight of a large herd of these huge Jurassic creatures must have been amazing.

Protecting the family

A family of **Brachiosaurus** fed quietly on a clump of trees. When they had eaten all the best leaves, they would then move on, trudging through the thick ferns.

Suddenly, an **Allosaurus** (<u>AL</u>-OH-<u>SAW</u>-RUS) ran out of the trees.

The small dinosaurs stayed close to their mothers, where it was safest. Meanwhile, the big males lumbered along beside them.

It chased a young **Brachiosaurus**. The **Allosaurus** was hungry. Its great jaws gaped open, showing long, sharp teeth.

It had not dared to attack an adult **Brachiosaurus**. Instead, it had gone straight for a young one, sinking its teeth into the soft neck.

The **Allosaurus** staggered, dropped the baby and tried to bite its tail as it struck again. The baby squealed before it died. **Brachiosaurus** had lost its young. It reared up on its back legs and crashed down its front legs on **Allosaurus'** head. The attacker fell to the ground, its skull crushed and its back badly broken. It, too, was now dead.

A big male **Brachiosaurus** turned and charged the **Allosaurus** as it dragged the baby away, whacking the predator with its tail.

Brachiosaurus data

Crane neck

Brachiosaurus had a very long neck. It could raise and lower it like a crane and swing it from side to side, using the strong muscles in its chest. The bones in its neck were hollow. This made them much lighter. Muscles stretching from its back and up its neck helped **Brachiosaurus** to hold its head up without much effort.

Brachiosaurus, with its long neck and massive body, was one of the largest dinosaurs ever to have walked on planet Earth. If you had been able to meet one, however, it would not have harmed you – unless you threatened it. This was because it did not eat meat but lived only on plants.

Powerful tail

Brachiosaurus' tail was long and powerful. It probably held it off the ground in a way that helped to balance the weight of its neck. **Brachiosaurus** may have used its tail as a weapon to fight off attacks by meat-eating dinosaurs.

Big nostrils

Just above this dinosaur's eyes, on top of its head, there were two very large nostrils.

Scientists once thought it needed these to breathe when in water. However, we now know it did not live in water most of the time. Instead, the nostrils may have been used for snorting noises, as signals to the herd, or to help cool it down by taking in large amounts of air. These large nostrils may also have given **Brachiosaurus** a good sense of smell.

Big feet

At the ends of **Brachiosaurus'** straight, thick legs were broad, round feet. You can count the number of toes it had. The toe bones in **Brachiosaurus'** front feet were a bit longer than those on the back feet, and more like the bones in a hand than a foot. For most of the time, it walked on its toes.

Useful stones

Because it had no grinding teeth, **Brachiosaurus** had to gulp its food whole. It swallowed small, rough stones, too. They helped to grind up the food in its stomach. But they soon became worn smooth. **Brachiosaurus** then spat them out and looked for more which it could swallow.

The Sauropod family

Brachiosaurus (1) belonged to a family, or group, of dinosaurs called **Sauropods.** They were all very large, and had long necks, heavy bodies and long tails. They lived in different parts of the world, but were all herbivores, feeding on trees and plants growing along river banks.

Camarasaurus, (KAM-AR-A-SAW-RUS) **(2)**, one of the smaller members of this family but still a giant, lived in the area we now call North America, about 145 million years ago. It looked very much like its cousins but its neck and tail were shorter, and its back legs were longer than its front ones.

Camarasaurus means 'chambered lizard'. It gets this name from the hollow spaces that scientists found in its long backbone.

Supersaurus, (SUPER-<u>SAW</u>-RUS) **(3)**, was even bigger than its cousin, **Brachiosaurus**. Its name means 'super lizard'. **Supersaurus** may be re-named when scientists find more of its bones and know more about this huge dinosaur.

But another **Sauropod, Ultrasaurus**, (<u>ULL</u>-TRA-<u>SAW</u>-RUS) **(4)**, may have been larger still than its cousin, **Supersaurus.** Its name means 'gigantic lizard' and it was possibly the biggest **Sauropod** of all.

Some of its bones were first discovered in Colorado, in the United States, only a few years before you were born. Scientists are still studying them.

First published 1993
by Parragon Book Service, Bristol

Text and illustrations copyright
© 1993 Quartz Editorial Services
112 Station Road, Edgware HA8 7AQ

ISBN 1–85813–333–5

Printed and bound in Great Britain by BPCC Paulton Books